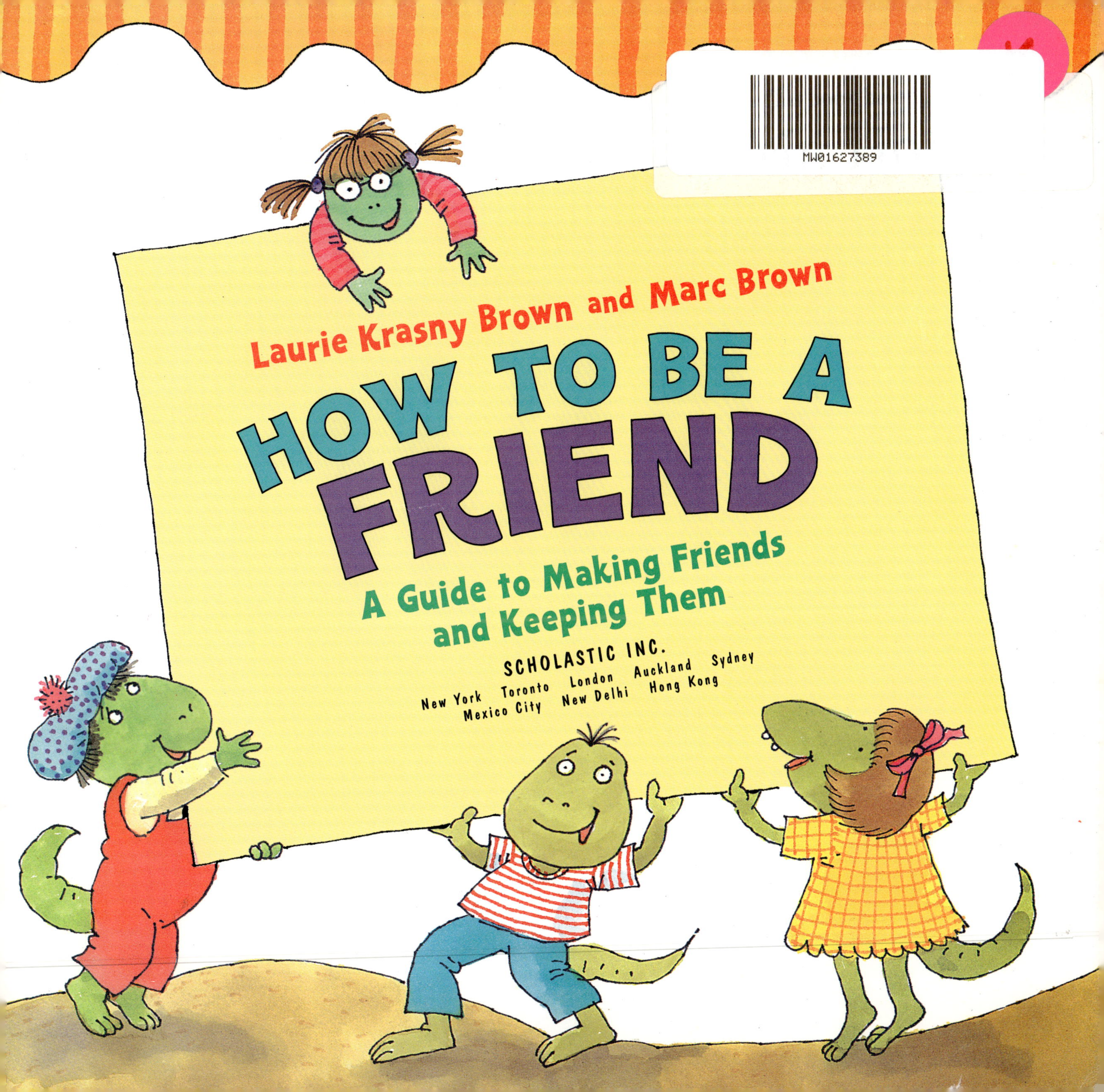
MW01627389
Laurie Krasny Brown and Marc Brown
HOW TO BE A
FRIEND
A Guide to Making Friends
and Keeping Them
SCHOLASTIC INC.
New York Toronto London Auckland Sydney
Mexico City New Delhi Hong Kong

For
Maria Modugno

Acknowledgments

Special thanks for their comments and criticism to our expert readers: Edwin Bartholomew, third grade teacher; Linda Braun, executive director of Families First Parenting Programs; Dorothy Burlage, Ph.D., clinical psychologist; Bernice Hawkins, second grade teacher; Phyllis Oppenheim, special education teacher; Polly Rizzotto, kindergarten teacher; Judie Stolp, head of lower school; Phyllis Wender, literary agent; and Denise Yocum, Psy.D., school counselor, Powell Associates.

ISBN 0-439-15399-9

Published by Scholastic Inc., 555 Broadway, New York, NY 10012, by arrangement with Little, Brown and Company (Inc.)
SCHOLASTIC and associated logos are trademarks and/or registered trademarks of Scholastic Inc.

12 11 10 9 8 7 6 5 4 3 2 1 9/9 0 1 2 3 4/0

Printed in the U.S.A. 09

First Scholastic printing, May 1999

Contents

Me, Myself, and I

There are times when it feels good to be by yourself, enjoying your own company.

You can think up ideas, pretend, and play exactly what you want.

With no one else around, you can have all the toys to yourself.

Who Can Be Your Friend?

But some games are too hard to play by yourself. And they're not as much fun all alone.

There are times when you may feel lonely or bored, when you want to have someone to play with.

Ummm . . . want to play?
Okay!

Anyone who is nice to you and who likes to play with you can become a friend.

Friends can be different from each other in all kinds of ways.

Hi! My name's Martha.
What's yours?

My baby-sitter is a friend.

He's my boyfriend.

I have a friend in sixth grade.
My friend speaks Spanish. ¿Habla español?
My friend has red hair. And freckles!
Please pass the chips.
Our friend lives next door.
My friend has a beard.

But there is one important way
that friends are always alike.

Friends feel the same way about each other!

Ways to Be a Friend

There are many ways to show that you like someone and want to be a friend.

You can protect a friend if someone starts bothering him.

You can play fair. Flip a coin with a friend to see who goes first.

You can share toys and other things.

You can stand up for friends, even when other kids complain about them or make fun of them.

You can invite them to play with you.

You can listen to your friends and pay attention to what they say.

You can try to cheer up a friend who's feeling sad.

You can offer help to friends when they need it.

You can cooperate. Go along with *your friend's* ideas sometimes.

Good jump!
You win!

You can compliment your friend, even when she wins and you lose. That's being a good sport.

You can keep your word. Then friends will know that they can trust you.

You can do things for friends, like making them special presents.

Joining in the Fun

Everyone feels left out sometimes. And it's not always easy to join in.

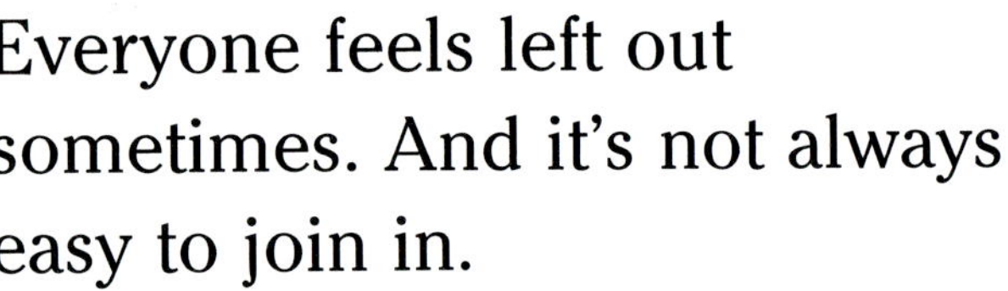

Feeling left out hurts inside. But acting too angry about it usually doesn't help.

Doing nothing isn't much help, either. You may end up feeling helpless and sad.

What you *can* do instead . . . is to invite someone else to play with you.

Or find something you like doing on your own for a while.

Later, you could try to join in the group again. If you watch to see what they are playing, you might be able to offer some help.

Feeling Shy

We all feel shy at times, such as when we meet new classmates or go to new places.

When you feel shy, it takes courage even to say hi to someone. But the more you practice, the easier it gets.

Ways *Not* to Be a Friend

Friends are bound to disagree about things. Even best friends can bother each other sometimes.

There are many ways to upset your friends.

No fair!
You're cheating!

If you cheat and don't follow the rules.

You Stupidosaurus!

Don't call me that!

If you insult them or call them mean names.

You can't play.
It's only for boys!

If you don't let them play.

Nya, nya—
na, na, na!

If you tease or make fun of them.

If you hit or hurt them.

If you don't share things.

If you don't let your friend play with anyone else.

If you act like a poor sport, showing off when you win or quitting so you won't lose.

If you blame friends for something they didn't do.

If you ignore what your friends say.

Bosses and Bullies

Being a boss means that you like to tell you friends what to do when you play. You like to make all the rules. But friends may get upset if you never let them have a chance to be in charge.

You be the sister.
You be the baby.
I'm the mom!

You're always the mom, Annie.
I want to decide this time!

Yeah, Annie.
Don't be so bossy!

One of the worst ways to treat a friend is to act like a bully and try to scare someone into doing what you want.

If someone bullies you, *try* not to get upset. Tell the bully to leave you alone. Join other, friendly kids. If that doesn't work, ask a grown-up for help.

Making Up with a Friend

There is always more than one way to settle an argument. If you and your friend want to use the same toy, what could you do instead of fighting over it?

Be creative. Think of a way you both can use it.

Decide to take turns.

Try to get enough toys for both of you.

Make a deal. If *you* get what you want, what can your friend have?

Use a trick such as flipping a coin or counting one-potato, two-potato to see who goes first.

Decide to play with something else.

Arguments
Arguments can make friends feel so angry, they can hardly think about making up . . . at least, not until they find a safe way to get out their anger.
1
You need some clouds.
Stop that! This is my side.
4
It's ruined! It's all your fault!
Nice picture of a storm.
5
It was supposed to be a sunny day.
Mine was, too.

2
See how you like it!
3
Oh, yeah? I'll show you!
6
7
Sorry.
That's okay. You're still my friend.

Sometimes an argument just gets worse and worse, angrier and angrier, with no end in sight. Friends may need to separate, take time out, or get some grown-up help.

Talking Out an Argument

Here are some steps to help you talk out an argument:

1 Stop arguing.

2 Calm down. Take deep breaths, count backwards, relax your muscles, or leave the group for a minute.

3 Agree to talk it out.

4 Everyone gets a turn to tell, not yell, their story and be listened to without interruptions.

5 Think up lots of ideas for solving the problem.

6 Try to choose the best solution, the one everyone agrees on and thinks will work.

7 Decide how to go about carrying out this plan.

8 Do it!

9 Remember, arguments are allowed, but meanness is not!

Remember:
In order to please everyone at least a little, you may not get exactly what you want.

Being Friendly

Being friendly means showing that you care about other kids, even the ones you hardly know. You can make them feel important and help them to belong.

It means treating others the way you would like them to treat you!

It feels great to have a friend!